DISCOVER YOUR KIDS GIFTS

Helping Your Kids To Know Their Gifts In Life

Table of contents

Chapter 1

Find your children's gifts

I have forever been astounded by how from the get-go in life kids start to show the extraordinary characters that God has given them. As guardians, you're most likely mindful that a few newborn children rest calmly in their bunks while others continually weep for consideration. You've additionally seen that a few little children joyfully play with their toys while others tire you out amidst their explorations. These early conduct contrasts that young people display are only a hint of something larger!

All along, no two youngsters are indistinguishable. Every youngster is a person with an unmistakable character and an elite mix of gifts and gifts that make them interestingly qualified to do the unique plans that God has for their lives. At the point when you join these natural characteristics with their unfurling valuable encounters, God has made them with a reason that no one but they can satisfy (Jeremiah 29:11).

God puts incredible worth on every one-of-a-kind individual He made.

He sees people uniquely in contrast to the world. That is the reason it's vital to such an extent that we as guardians, educators, coaches and good examples assist our kids with seeing

exactly how exceptional they are in God's eyes!
The following are a couple of significant Sacred texts to impart to your youngsters to assist them with seeing exactly the amount God loves them and the amount He esteems their remarkable gifts:
Before I framed you in the womb
I knew you,
before you were born I separated
you…
For you made my deepest being;
you see me together in my mom's
belly
I acclaim you since I'm
frightfully and brilliantly made;
your works are brilliant, I realise
that without a doubt.
My edge was not stowed away
from you
at the point when I was made in
the mystery place,
at the point when I was woven
together in the profundities of the
earth.
Your eyes saw my unformed
body;
every one of the days appointed
for me was written in your book
before one of them became.

Each wonderful gift is from a higher place.
Some portion of our positions as guardians is to assist our youngsters with distinguishing, sustaining, and expressing their gifts in manners that give them pleasure and favour their families, chapels, and networks.
Train up a kid in the manner he ought to go, and when he is old he won't withdraw from it.
The following are a couple of significant things we can do to help our youngsters perceive and foster their inherent gifts:
At the point when our kid communicates an interest in specific exercises, we can give them potential chances to investigate them!
At the point when our kid shows a fitness or gift in specific regions, we can assist them with creating it!
At the point when our kid welcomes us to partake in exercises they love, we can focus on investing energy with them!
As we watch our youngsters create, we can give careful consideration to the things that they succeed at — the things that

they appear to have a characteristic fitness for — and the manners by which they normally express their gifts. We can see how they collaborate with others and tune in for affirmation from others about the things that we are noticing.

The signs we uncover when they are youthful will assist them with finding how they fit into the collection of Christ and how they can best utilise their profound gifts to serve the congregation as they develop!

Some of the time good-natured guardians fall into the snare of coming down on their youngsters to satisfy hopes that God never planned them to satisfy! The following are a couple of parental ways of behaving we ought to keep away from:

Contrasting our kids with others - particularly companions and kin - regardless of how good-natured those examinations might be! We must regard every one of our kids as the special people that they are. Examinations are just a variety of disdain, desire, and competition.

Attempting to encounter the things we passed up in our lives as youngsters by constraining our children to seek after things they have no fitness for or interest in! Every one of us has one life to live. We mustn't attempt to carry on with our lives through our youngsters yet rather assist them with making every second count! Compelling our kids to emulate our example! We might fantasise about passing down the privately-run company or seeing our youngster go to our institute of matriculation - yet isn't it more significant for us to bring up kids who are seeking after the way that God has put them on?
As our kids mature and follow Christ, we can assist them with finding their profound gifts and utilising them to fortify, empower, and develop the nearby church.
Every one of you ought to utilise anything that presents you have gotten to serve others, as steadfast stewards of God's beauty in its different structures.
- 1 Peter 4:10
Bringing up kids who perceive their one-of-a-kind gifts and

appreciate imparting them to others is a gift that everybody benefits from!

Assuming you are searching for a rousing kids' book that will assist you with acquainting your small kids with the idea of how extraordinary they are and the exceptional gifts that they have, I can imagine no better determination

How old were your kids when you initially started to see their extraordinary gifts? How have you seen their gifts foster after some time? Kindly offer your accounts in the remarks!

Chapter 2

Know your children's spiritual gifts

For one thing, an otherworldly gift isn't a characteristic ability or capacity with which we are conceived

an office, position, or occupation any of us hold or may hold from now on

working in a particular topographical area

an extraordinary inclination for managing individuals of specific ages.

Profound gifts permit devotees to perform explicit undertakings past the domain of their human expertise and capacity. Each individual who has placed their confidence in Jesus Christ gets these gifts from God. Each devotee has something like one profound gift. You'll find in the wake of taking the profound gifts test that while not a solitary one of us has every one of the gifts, a few devotees might have multiple.

The Essence of God circulates these gifts as He sees fit, for His motivation. Every one of us gets the specific gift God believes us should have, as you'll see when you take the profound gifts test. His elegance alone gives these gifts to us. They aren't a consequence of an individual's development level, or because we mentioned a particular gift through supplication, or given an individual's broad training. While there's no thorough rundown of otherworldly gifts, you can find six halfway records in the New Confirmation. Peruse the accompanying entries with your youngster to get an overall outline of the profound gifts referenced and their motivations in God's congregation today. Whether all profound gifts are accessible today is a dubious issue in some congregation customs. Thus, after taking the profound gifts test with your family, make certain to look for counsel from your minister, youth pioneer, or otherworldly coach as you assist your kid with finding their otherworldly gift. While every devotee gets this "gift" from God, the object isn't so we can involve it for our advantage. Furthermore, carrying consideration or brilliance to ourselves is not. God gives every one of us these Profound gifts so we can help other people. That remembers those for the neighbourhood church where we join in and the people who are essential for the widespread

Church enveloping all adherents all over the planet. The reason for each gift is to assist the local area of adherents with working better. It's additionally to complete the service of imparting Christ to our stinging world. That is the reason there's no space for harshness, desire, pride, or contrasting ourselves with others while we're practising our gift. There's no such thing as a "superfluous" or "insignificant" gift by the same token. Indeed, a few gifts are more "in front of an audience" and noticeable while others are more "in the background" and less perceived. That is only how God expected it to be. If it's not too much trouble, now, the presence of an otherworldly gift doesn't resist any of us from transgression. We're dependent upon frustration, narrow-mindedness, adolescence, sluggishness, abusing our gifts, blemishes, and blunder. Keep in mind that we as a whole are made of mud. Although gifts are given to every one of us at the hour of salvation (most frequently separated from the adherent's mindfulness), the manifestation of that gift is cognizant. It's accomplished as the Essence of God controls the adherent. It depends on every one of us to find, create and practise our gift. As a parent, you can help your kid in this revelation, improvement, and exercise process.

This connection will take you to a self-scoring Otherworldly Gifts Test and Stock. Begin the excursion today with your kid and assist that person with finding their otherworldly giving. Incidentally, if you haven't yet explained your otherworldly gift as a parent, carve out an opportunity to learn together as you take the profound gifts test. It's an incredible approach to coach your kid regardless of their age in a dccp scnsc.

As well as finishing the profound gift stock, you'll perceive your youngster's gift as they experience it. Urge your kid to engage in a wide range of chapel and local area exercises — more than sports or music. Then, at that point, support their inclusion. At the point when you see your kid succeed in something, observe and tell them you saw it as well.

Your kid's profound gift might be clear from the get-go. Or on the other hand, it may not turn out to be completely known until their adolescent years or significantly later. Try not to allow your youngster to become deterred on the off chance that their gift isn't clear immediately, even after taking the profound gifts test. Assist your kid with showing restraint. Keep on asking with your kid and keep your hearts and brains open. Ultimately, they will find their profound gift and fill in their capacity to utilise their gifts to extol God.

A while back, I worked with an otherworldly gifts service in my congregation. Under the management of our minister, we attempted to assist with recognizing profound gifts in the individuals from our assemblage and to assist them with tracking down spots to connect into administration the Collection of Christ. Rather than taking individuals who detested working with children and causing them to be Sunday Teachers since it was their "turn" or requesting that individuals be simply one more warm body in a congregation chamber, we looked to match interests, otherworldly gifts, and development levels with proper positions. This approach gave me an irresistible craving to recognize and confirm the assortment of otherworldly gifts that God has put in His body. Although I frequently consider how this connects with my congregation, I have started to contemplate what otherworldly gifts mean to the family and how they can uncover God's calling to every Christian. I'm composing fundamentally from the focal point of spouse and mother, yet I fccl that what I nccd to say could connect with people and the people who don't yet have kids also. We all have a family or local area of companions, family members, and individual family in Christ whom we are assembled to support and work with.

As I take a gander at my significant other and two

children (a five-year-old young lady and a child kid), I can see extraordinary character qualities, interests, and profound gifts that God has put inside them. At times it's quite simple to focus on the manners in which they are unique about me. However, in 1 Corinthians 12, Paul brings up that God has deliberately made every one of us remarkable. He never expected us to be in every way the equivalent. Rather, His main goal is satisfied through contrastingly gifted individuals cooperating to achieve a similar reason.

Although there can be some slight variations between arrangements of profound gifts, these are the fundamental sections to which Book of scriptures researchers will generally turn: 1 Corinthians 12:8-10, 28; Romans 12:6-8; Ephesians 4:11; and 1 Peter 4:9-10.

Following is a rundown of the gifts tracked down in these entries alongside certain clues or hints on how they could begin to appear in a kid. The more seasoned your youngster is, the more clear things will be as their character structures and concrete. Notwithstanding, I see a portion of similar character qualities in my girl today as I did when she was an infant. Profound skill varies from character here and there, yet since God made all aspects of us, these things are in discussion with one another. What fun it is to see a little individual unfurling like a blossom and to perceive how God is functioning in them! Remember that God is astonishing and thus frequently involves us despite our innate capacities so He could gain esteem! While our gifts might tell part of the narrative of God's approaching our life, they may not uncover the entire story. They are, nonetheless, an extraordinary spot to begin.

Chapter 3

Know your kids spiritual talents

Pretty much every parent peering down at their infant is considering what abilities this little beloved newborn has brought along.

The interest is frequently hard to contain and most guardians need to be aware as soon as conceivable what gifts their little one has so they can support those gifts and be pleased guardians of a wonder.

A few guardians truly do observe that their youngsters are wonders.

However, many find that their youngsters have next to no genuine ability. Furthermore, this revelation fills them with a sensation of overpowering frustration.

More terrible still, many guardians see flashes of ability in their youngsters - however, the sparkles don't keep going long to make the shine of accomplishment. Furthermore, this leads guardians to dissatisfaction notwithstanding disillusionment.

These sensations of dissatisfaction and disappointment are barely noticeable on occupied school days when everybody is in a hurry. Yet, they come to torment guardians during getaways and school breaks.

At the point when they glance around and find that companions and partners have skilled kids, they want to dive into their kid and scratch out something that seems to be an ability.

This makes excursions upsetting for both parents and youngsters. Furthermore, any ability which might have existed is lost in the pressure.

Is it true that you are a parent who is feeling the strain to find and support your kid's gifts and assets? I'm sharing a bit-by-bit plan that you can use to find your kid's gifts and assets in this article.

What is an Ability

Ability is the innate capacity to accomplish something well - particularly without being educated.

This is the meaning of ability from the Cambridge English word reference.

When you read this definition - you fall into the snare of reasoning that ability is an innate quality. Also, similar to a great many different guardians - this legend fools you into needing to open up your kid's cerebrum and see what gifts your kid is concealing inside their mind.

In any case, it is significant not to fall into this snare.

The best-misguided judgement about ability is that kids are brought into the world with it.

No, they are not.

You can't dive into your kid's psyche and track down your kid's gifts - regardless of how determined you might be as a parent.

You need to permit your kid's gifts to arise by establishing the right climate.

Gifts in a real sense jump out of youngsters when the circumstances are correct.
They are practically similar to saplings that jump out of the ground when the ground is soggy after a spell of a downpour.
If you are attempting to find your kid's ability - stop now.
Regardless of whether you dig you will just track down the seed - and it will be impossible for you to transform it into the strong tree that it is intended to be.
In any case, assuming that you establish the right climate your kid's ability will arise. Also, assuming you continue to support it, it will develop.
The one thing that truly prompts kids to investigate their abilities is weariness.
At the point when a kid sits around aimlessly, with no place to go and no wellspring of diversion, you will find your kid starting to do "something".
Furthermore, when you stroll in - you will have a kid anxious to show you what they have realised or fairly found about themselves.

Try not to begin hollering at your kid for having left the seat when you taught them to stay there until you returned

Respect what your kid has achieved. Also, urge them to accomplish more. The excursion towards investigating abilities begins when your youngster is exhausted. Also, proceed when you show interest and give out consolation.

The barrier as of now is your assumption about your thought process is an important ability. If you are a musician and believe your kid should dominate the piano, you might track down their cartwheels as pointless and an exercise in futility. What's more, if you say this - your kid will neither end up a musician nor a tumbler.

If you can't see any abilities in your kid, start to search for qualities.

Indeed - abilities are not the same as qualities.

Ability is execution arranged. It is something your kid does that you can see.

A strength, then again, is a piece of your youngster's personality.

You may not see it except if you are effectively searching for it. What's more, you are particularly prone to miss it and even consider the strength a negative quality in your kid except if you are cautiously looking at how you think.

For instance, half a month prior, a parent contacted me to ask me how he ought to change his child's nice and loosened-up disposition about everything.

He was concerned that his child would grow up to be imprudent and unmotivated to take on difficulties.

I assisted him with seeing that nice can likewise be called cool-headed and can be excellent during stress when things turn out badly.

Furthermore, very soon this stressed Father thought of a circumstance, in which the quality that he hated so much in his child, had held them in great stead.

He related an episode where he had crashed into his thought process was a shallow puddle on a blustery day. The puddle was a lot further than he had suspected, and the vehicle began sinking. Being an individual who was accustomed to doing things right… on time… .and impeccably… this present circumstance tossed him into a condition of frenzy and self-fault and shut down his reasoning cerebrum.

Due to his laidback mentality, he was prone to rescue circumstances when things were not working out in a good way. When he understood what was going on - he leaped out of the vehicle - asked the vehicles behind them to back up and incited his Father to turn around with full power.

This saved the vehicle and their lives that day.

As we talked this Father acknowledged how supporting his child's capacity to be prudent in unpleasant conditions could be a gigantic resource. If by some stroke of good luck he could quit zeroing in on being agreeable as a negative quality.

A strength is character quality. It may not be noticeable because it isn't expertise based however arises in all that a kid does. Dissimilar to gifts, we might have to look cautiously before we track down a youngster's assets. Furthermore, as indicated by popular specialist Lea Waters - on the off chance that we search for qualities under the accompanying general gatherings - we are bound to track down them

Consider a capable individual and you make certain to observe that one of these personal qualities is an unmistakable piece of their character

A fruitful financial specialist like Jack Mama of Ali Baba couldn't ever have prevailed without fortitude...

These individuals had abilities. However, thcsc abilitics would be futile without their remarkable personal assets.

A strength is something that easily falls into place for your kid. Something encourages your kid. Furthermore, it along these lines becomes something your youngster decides to do frequently.

Having brought up three little girls, I can affirm as a specialist witness that kid-raising is much harder than marriage. However, a lot of guardians make it significantly harder than they need to. They're undeniably stressed and busied over doing a lot of things they think will work on the possibilities of their child "ending up" OK.

Meanwhile, they overlook or slight the main things, which to my psyche reduce to four things: assisting their kid show up at adulthood with a moderately solid close-to-home life (feeling like they have a place, that they matter, that they're cherished, that they can trust); having a significant relationship with Lord of some kind; having respectable training; and having a decent handle of their centre assets — their talent — to make a commitment to the world and make money. If guardians just gave their kids those four things, those kids would have the majority of what they need to flourish as a grown-up.

While I care profoundly about pretty much every one of the four

of those activities, my work centres around the fourth one — assisting individuals with grasping their centre assets. What might you at any point do as a parent to assist your kid with valuing their talent?
So when would it be advisable for you to begin attempting to distinguish your kid's talent? The second they're conceived. You will not have the option to see a lot. So don't stretch out beyond the kid. Simply expect it's there and welcome it by telling that little individual how pleased you are about their appearance.
Then, at that point, you pause and watch. Since there won't be a ton to see from the start, you might be enticed to lose interest, particularly if you're the dad. Moms are honoured with maternal senses about their kids, so they will generally see the indications of personhood a ton sooner.
The way to notice the talent of your kid is to focus on their energy. Where do they invest their effort? What exercises make them wake up, to get truly intrigued, to zero in on the

errand? What holds their consideration? What exercises do they readily participate in for significant periods (other than casual exercises like sitting in front of the television)? Which ones would they like to continue to return to? Energy in a kid is an indication that something is enacting their skill.

You can't quickly understand what that something is. So anything you do, for about the initial 12 years of your kid's life, stay with perceptions of their way of behaving and avoid understanding it.

Since your kid asks to begin piano examples doesn't mean they have dreams of turning into a professional piano player. Their inspiration might be to accomplish something their companions are doing.

Moreover, when your eighth-grader gives a discourse and gets chosen class president, that doesn't mean she's fated for a day-to-day existence in governmental issues. Her talent might be tied in with shaping connections, thus she got chosen since she was the main candidate that everybody at her school knew.

Never drive your kid into a way. Rather, see what way is by all accounts arising for them. See what seems to give them energy, and afterward, feed that energy. I call that respecting the gift. You attempt to work with your kid's talent, not block it or baffle it. That can be difficult to do, particularly when their skill separates fundamentally from your own. I see that regularly with a very effective and whose dad's talent displays power. He's an objective-situated, results-driven person who knows how to set an arrangement, execute it, and win. In the meantime, he has a child who lives in the realm of ideas. Today the kid is truly into fractals. In any case, a couple of months after the fact he's investing all his energy investigating the acoustics of instruments. In any case, that diminishes when he finds chess. Thus it goes. Anything the kid does, he does as such enthusiastically. In any case, his interests continue to change.

Presently you can envision how disappointed his dad should be. He continues to ask his child to define objectives. "You're never going to go anyplace without an objective and an arrangement," he tells him. However, prepare to be blown away. The young fellow isn't attempting to "get" anyplace! That is not in his persuasive cosmetics. He's on a scholarly odyssey, investigating what to him appears to be a perpetually entrancing world. There is no objective. There's just the excursion. The dad will possibly demolish him assuming that he attempts to compel him to start acting responsibly and adjust to the dad's concept of what is important throughout everyday life (which is driven by the dad's skill).

So imagine a scenario where no obvious "way" is by all accounts arising for your youngster. Then as the parent, grow the universe of potential outcomes. Give your kid openness to various sorts of exercises, encounters, and conditions as could be expected.

As they go through those minutes, focus on their energy. Simply perceive how they answer. Indeed, even circumstances that you believe are immaterial (like your family getting your life partner at the air terminal), routine (like making supper), or even horrendous (like the demise of a relative), may uncover significant hints about your kid's skill. To be sure, skill is particularly uncovered in the ordinary, and in what your youngster does when they get to pick the movement. As my partners and I like to say: With regards to spotting skills, everything is proof.
One method for catching your perceptions is to keep a straightforward diary on your kid. You can composc a passage at whatever point you notice something fascinating, along the lines of "Today my kid partook in a play at school and completely cherished it. She said she particularly preferred it when everybody giggled after she introduced her line." Or, "Today my kid had a woodwind presentation. She didn't rehearse

for it how she should, yet when it came time to perform, she blew everyone's mind. I was flabbergasted." Or, "I can't get my kid to put down the book he began pursuing yesterday on the Nationwide conflict. He's simply caught up in it!"

If you gather those sorts of passages north for quite a long while, you'll wind up with a significant group of information from which to begin reaching a few determinations about your kid's skill. You'll begin to see a few subjects and examples rehashing the same thing. Then you'll be in a superior situation to assist your kid with beginning to become mindful of and claiming their assets and interests.

You can likewise keep an arrangement of your kid's achievements, particularly the ones that they, by their confirmation, truly delighted in and are truly glad for. That assortment could incorporate things they've made, stories or papers they've composed, keepsakes of different undertakings they've had or accomplishments they treasure, and particularly photographs, recordings, and additionally sound accounts of them doing their "thing" or depicting some occasion they saw as particularly invigorating.

Frankly, I don't know that assisting your youngster with awakening their talent takes significantly more than that. It's tied in with noticing first, then over the long run starting to perceive a few repeating subjects and ways of behaving, then directing out those subjects toward your kid and certifying them as important resources, and afterward commending your youngster's achievements when they feel they've gotten along nicely. (Coincidentally, it is not decent — as a matter of fact, it's hurtful — to let your kid know that all that they do is astounding, phenomenal, the best of all time. Allow them to let you know what they view as significant and fulfilling.)

Precepts 22:6 expresses, "Train up a youngster up a kid in the manner he ought to go … In any event, when he is old he won't withdraw from it." The words "train up" come from animating a sense of taste for, making a preference for, and fostering a longing for. The words "in the manner in which he ought to go" allude to the inherent bowing of the kid, their regular demeanour, and the "way" God has made them.

So, this saying orders guardians to focus on their youngster's talent and assist them with embracing it, owning it, and becoming an expert at utilising it. I can't envision a higher honour — to get a little individual who is an endowment of God to the world, and afterward to gradually, cautiously, yet purposefully oversee the opening up of that gift so they can complete the "benevolent acts" that have been arranged from endlessness for them to do.

Chapter 4

Understanding Your Children's Spiritual Gifts

Then being genial and good-natured is your kid's solidarity. What's more, an extraordinary quality should be supported because it is the main quality of cooperation and initiative.

Moving away from a battle is certainly not an indication of the shortcoming as you naturally suspect but an indication of compassion and high profound remainder.

No. Keeping away from conflicts isn't fainthearted. Superfluously diving into battles constantly is an exercise in futility and best stayed away from. What's more, is an indication of shrewdness.

So the method for finding your kid's assets is

To painstakingly notice

To reconsider assumptions

It is essential to comprehend that the piece of ability that is not set

in stone by qualities, or as such is in-conceived, is "interest".
Your kid will be keener on certain things than on others. Interest is significant because it will provoke your youngster to zero in additional on those things than others. For instance - Assuming your kid is keen on music, they will zero in on the melody significantly more than you will. They will get complexities in the tune and beat more than you. Subsequently, when they attempt to sing - they will sing superior to you since they have more information around there.

Whenever they have endeavoured it and found that they are great at it assuming you energise them and show interest in seeing a more ideal form of the tune, they will start to rehearse it.

When a kid begins rehearsing they are probably going to surrender, since training is exhausting and includes adapting to disappointment and not getting deterred by it. On the off chance that you are involved, you can assist them with keeping the

bigger picture in view and stay zeroed in on the objective without getting deterred.
When your kid arrives at a specific degree of capability in specific expertise, they will need to work on it further. Also, assuming that you are involved, you can assist your kid with viewing as on the web or disconnected assets to gain from (contingent upon their learning style). Continuously recollect that getting the hang of something is difficult, and there will be barricades here that you should rouse your kid to survive.
When the kid figures out how to explore the space of that ability - you can gradually remove little strides from the genuine learning and take an interest just however much your kid wants. Be there however don't rule the scene.
That is the best way to deal with propelling without compressing.
. Permit Your Kid to Get Exhausted
One of the greatest impediments to finding an ability or perceiving a strength - is an extreme diversion.

At the point when youngsters who are generally bustling the entire day - out of nowhere have nothing to do during a planned or unscheduled break - they alarm. They call this absence of activities exhausting.
What's more, as guardians this causes us to feel regretful and we hurry to fix their fatigue with amusement.
We hand them gadgets that offer detached amusement
Or on the other hand, we sign them up for classes that propel them to do things a specific way at a specific time.
Also, with this, we kill their inspiration.
Gadgets kill inspiration in light of how they hack the Dopamine pathway of the cerebrum. Also, exercises kill inspiration since they depend on guidance and execution.
Permit your kid to get exhausted
Give your youngster the existence to concentrate without being surged.
The main thing to be tossed to the breezes throughout a break - constrained or in any case is standard and discipline.

The greater part of us believes that the shortfall of routine and discipline is an opportunity and we envision that by abandoning the everyday practice of the house we have liberated our youngsters to investigate themselves.

Be that as it may, this is a misinterpretation

Routine and discipline are critical because they save time from routine exercises and assist youngsters with setting aside the opportunity to venture out. A normal causes youngsters to have a real sense of reassurance and strong as a result of the feeling of control and consistency that it offers. Furthermore, it is just when youngsters have a good sense of reassurance that they can practise their highcr mental capabilities.

In a house where routine and discipline are followed, youngsters are liberated to arrive at their actual potential.

Hit the hay and wake up simultaneously consistently

Serve quality dinners on timeMore than whatever else -

youngsters need to feel associated with their folks.
if you simply pass on your kid to do what they need and get engrossed in the thing you are doing - you will find your kid has tracked down their direction to a gadget trying to find an association or to shut out the absence of association.
Permit youngsters their spare energy to do what they please - yet not the entire day for a long time.
Interface at eating times and sleep time and pay attention to what they need to say.
Give loads of love to support your presence for the day.
Motivate As opposed to Training
Continually instructing your youngster. And afterward irritating your kid about not doing what you asked, is the certain fire method for killing inspiration.
Advise yourself that your kid will lead you to their ability or strength. You can't lead them to it by jabbing and pushing them.
Your job is to move, not to educate.

Make energy of excitement and enterprising nature in the house by accomplishing something yourself. It doesn't need to be something you maintain that your kid should do. Notwithstanding, it should be something that you are energetic about. Your kid should see you taking a stab at it whether it is heating up or earthenware or whatever else. Also, enduring regardless of the multitude of snags without fretting over the disappointment. At the point when your kid sees you so dedicated and motivated - they will be enlivened to begin and persevere with something themselves.

Switch off the television and avoid gadgets. Tragically in a lot of houses, the common energy is one of being irritated and disturbed in light of fatigue. Also, this is helped by keeping the television running behind the scenes giving aloof amusement. At the point when detached diversion is with such ease accessible your kid is probably not going to strive to accomplish

something to get the Dopamine hurry to feel compensated.
One of the simplest ways of deterring your kid from doing anything is to start contrasting them and different youngsters. Tragically for the majority of us, the examination is a lifestyle. Also, we feel that contrasting kids is the best inspiration device.
In any case, we should understand that it isn't.
When you start to contrast your kid and another kid, you pass on to your kid that "I feel that kid is superior to you."
"I will adore you provided that you become like that kid."
Furthermore, by conveying these unbending assumptions - you guarantee that your kid is demotivated. Furthermore, I am reluctant to attempt.
Furthermore, a kid who is reluctant to attempt is probably not going to at any point track down an ability or a strength and succeed at anything.
Most kids are hesitant to endeavour anything new because they fear disappointment.

Inquisitively, anxiety toward disappointment is something youngsters are not brought into the world with. It is something that they gain from us their folks throughout some period.
A youngster who is figuring out how to walk has no clue that tumbling down while endeavouring to walk is an indication of disappointment.
In any case, throughout some undefined time frame, the message is crashed into their cerebrum.
"If another kid figures out how to swim or compose or skate or show improvement over you - you are a disappointment." They are told.
The strain of continuously contending, continuously attempting to win, is unplcasant to such an extent that kids conclude that it could be simpler not to attempt.
At the point when you invest a great deal of energy with one another throughout a break, both you and your kid will begin irritating one another.
While your kid might not have the opportunity to call attention

to this to you. As a parent, you are probably going to get the chance to tick your kid off each time they accomplish something that irritates you.

Also, in my experience guardians are neither careful nor delicate when they are irritated.

Assuming the entire day is spent quarrelling about little issues - you will observe that tiny things have been achieved by your kid in light of an absence of inspiration and the feeling of dread toward struggle.

Assuming you feel set off by your kid's way of behaving, look at your response to the trigger and figure out why you respond how you do.

Comprehend that contention won't go anyplace, however assuming you answer as opposed to responding - you will want to assist your kid with finding their solidarity.

Rather than saying - "You need to stand by listening to me if not you will be rebuffed " On the off chance that you say "Might you at any point help out me how do you help out your companions when you want to play a match?

Then, at that point, we can partake in the day."
This assists your kid with finding an inward strength and a method for utilising it for their potential benefit.
Recall that abilities are pointless without internal qualities that assist us with sharpening those gifts and succeeding at them. Likewise recall that it is more vital to find internal qualities than to perform and win prizes for gifts. Since internal qualities - like versatility for instance - perform various tasks for us in all that we do. While an ability like having the option to move might have restricted utility.
As guardians, our objective ought to be to empower the advancement of confidence and inspiration in our kids so they can succeed in anything they endeavour.
In our frenzy to take down the opposition and guarantee that our youngsters have resumes loaded with grants for their different gifts, we should not permit ourselves to neglect to focus on this vital objective.

Chapter 5

Pray alongside your kids

The sobering news about bringing up kids is that we truly have no extreme command about whether our youngsters will pick the tight door that prompts life (Matthew 7:14) or the wide entryway that prompts annihilation. On the off chance that different encounters in life have not lowered us and shown us how subordinate we are to God, then, at that point, nurturing a pre-juvenile or teen will. Understanding our urgent need to rely upon God is uplifting news. When we surrender the innocent thought that we guardians can direct the decisions our youngsters will make and the profound door they will stroll through — tight or wide — then we are prepared to slip on the

knee cushions and quit fooling around with supplication.
What did we find out about supplication for our kids as they arranged for and entered puberty?
Ask routinely. Bring each worry, dream, and want about your youngster to God in an intense, relentless petition. (Luke 18:1-8 contains an extraordinary story on determined supplication that probably was for guardians of teens.)
Two of the best times to supplicate with your kid are heading to school (expecting you to drive the person in question) and at sleep time — paying little mind to progress in years. We lived around five miles from the school our youngsters went to when they were growing up. Each day we would ask about things generally essential to our kids — tests, companions, instructors, exercises. As the vehicle bested the slope just before the school building, we generally closed with a similar solicitation: "And Master, we ask that you would keep every one of our kids from mischief,

malevolence, and enticement this day, that they would encounter You at work in their lives and be involved by You to impact others for Your Realm. So be it." When our young people started to drive themselves to school, we would bring breakfast for this request time.

Sleep time petitions to heaven can be more private for every kid. Appeal to God for her future mate, connections, exercises, difficulties, allurements, and heart for God. Try not to expect that a teen is too enormous for you to stoop close to his bed and stroke his face and implore. Supplicate disagreeably. Before your kid hits puberty, appeal to God for his companion bunch — that he will have no less than one in number Christian pal for the high school years. Request that God shield your kid day to day from other people who might be a detestable impact. Additionally, consider requesting that God assist you with recognizing your kid doing things right so you can energise him in pursuing the ideal decisions.

Supplicate protectively. Over and over we looked for the Master's assistance in eliminating a companion or sketchy person from our youngster's life.
Every once in a while we would feel that one of our teenagers may be deluding us, yet we would never be sure beyond a shadow of a doubt. In those circumstances, we requested that God assist us with getting him assuming he had been accomplishing something wrong. God appears to feel frustrated about guardians who ask this request!
Ask with a burning intensity. One of the most misconstrued profound disciplines of the Christian life is petitioning God for fasting the surrendering of nourishment for a recommended time frame. Even though fasting doesn't procure focus with God, He in any case expects in Sacred text that we will quickly and implore (see Matthew 6:16-18) and vows to compensate us assuming we do it accurately.
We know a couple who might save every Monday to quick, sunup until twilight, and petition

God for their striving 14-year-old kid.

Supplicate when God carries your kid to mind. It could be at that exact instant, that your youngster is confronting a situation of basic significance. A few companions of our own felt areas of strength for an unexpected need one night to petition God for their girl. At the very time they got up and to their knees, a squad car was driving by their little girl's vehicle on a far-off mountain street where she and a sweetheart had gone to take a gander at the city lights, eat a sandwich, and talk. Obscure to them, he got away from a detainee who was concealed under the vehicle. The detainee was captured, and the young ladies drove off safe.

Ask your kid. It's simple for a petition to turn into a restrictive exchange — you and God. Why not do what one mother, Nina, did with her high school little girl, Natalie, and become petitioning God's accomplices? Natalie's high school years were loaded up with exceptional minutes in which she and her mother stooped together and supplicated over Natalie's battles and difficulties.

Ask all together. For more than 40 years of marriage, we have finished every day in petition altogether. No profound discipline has safeguarded our marriage and our family more than this day-to-day season of fellowship along with God.

Each of our six kids has now come to adulthood. Now that immaturity is behind us, you could think we are enticed to drift to the end goal. Barely! We kept on supplicating like never before for our youngsters even after the tempestuous juvenile years — despite everything.

God needs the same thing for yourself as well as your kid. Converse with Him. James 5:16 tells us, "The viable petition of an equitable man can achieve a lot."

A considerable lot of us likely believe it's smart, from a certain perspective, to supplicate with our children at sleep time. As we wrap our kids up, besides the fact that request can be a quieting schedule, it likewise instructs them that they can chat with the Divine force of the universe whenever and that he is close. However, we might be uncertain of what we ought to implore them about. Besides, when we're canine drained or the children are nearly an implosion, it's not difficult to get deterred and surrender together.

We frequently get demotivated when our ideal doesn't coordinate with the real world. Since we can't get six things separated from our daily agenda we wind up sitting idle. We can't get an entire hour at the exercise centre so we don't go. However, we'd frequently be in an ideal situation if we dealt with no less than a certain something, or got in 20-30 minutes of an exercise. The equivalent is valid here. For 1,000 reasons, it may very well be not great to implore with your children at a given time. However, something is normally not all that great, but not terrible either. Also, this prompts the following point.

My children are not prone to sit mindfully for extensive periods with heads bowed and a delicate shine radiating from their saintly countenances. Of course, I have issues as a grown-up staying on track with my requests. So while I unquestionably need to show my children regard for God, I breathe easy in light of the way that the Book of scriptures doesn't instruct that the length of our request is straightforwardly related to its profound importance (all things considered, the Ruler's Request is short). It's normally best to keep things brief and forthright, and afterward trust God to utilise them.

Will your children block you out assuming you supplicate the same things constantly? Perhaps. On the other hand, you most likely still recall a ton of the things that your folks rehashed to you again and again. (There are times I could want to fail to remember my father saying, "Assuming a task merits doing, it merits doing well.") Assuming something is significant — like having a heart that follows and confides in Jesus — then I wouldn't fret petitioning God for it a ton, both for me and for them. Doing so makes it more probable that your children will embrace that significance for themselves over the long haul. Many guardians have had the astounding/sentencing/humiliatin g experience of seeing their, ahem, not exactly advantageous activities imitated by their children. (It tends to be lowering for my significant other and me to stand by listening to our children play pretend with anything including a mother or daddy.) Turns out children can undoubtedly display our terrible way of behaving. Yet, fortunately, children can undoubtedly display beneficial things also. Also, you're the quickest and most successful model your kids have. Seeing you talking to God with them on a predictable premise will demystify the demonstration of petitioning God for your children and go quite far toward assisting them with laying out it as a propensity in their own lives. One thing I've done once in a while (and that I might want to accomplish a greater amount of) is to request that my children share one thing they're grateful for or potentially one thing they need to request that God assist them with. This assists jokes with seeing the genuine connection between supplication and their regular day-to-day existences (and it gives you as a parent a superior thought of what your kid is invigorated or stressed over — which could illuminate your requests). Likewise, go ahead and request that your children do the imploring. Once more, when you ask them reliably, you'll show them how to do this as a matter of course.

What I most need for my children — more than finding real success at school, finding a decent line of work, having their very own group, and so on — is for them to confide in and follow Jesus. So when I supplicate with them, my requests reliably mirror that. I can't change their hearts, however, God can.

www.ingramcontent.com/pod-product-compliance
Lightning Source LLC
LaVergne TN
LVHW052104160826
845678LV00015B/3347

* 9 7 9 8 8 4 9 9 4 2 8 1 0 *